METAMORPHOSIS

Poetry and Photos of a Grief Journey

NANCY J NELSON

Balboa Press books may be ordered through booksellers or by contacting:

Balboa Press
A Division of Hay House
1663 Liberty Drive
Bloomington, IN 47403
www.balboapress.com
1 (877) 407-4847

ISBN: 978-1-9822-1989-5 (sc)
ISBN: 978-1-9822-1990-1 (e)

Library of Congress Control Number: 2019901245

Print information available on the last page.

Balboa Press rev. date: 02/15/2019

BALBOA
PRESS
A DIVISION OF HAY HOUSE

METAMORPHOSIS

Poetry and Photography
of A Grief Journey

By Nancy J. Nelson

The poetry in this book explore the emotions I experienced during the first few months following my husband, Jay's death from lung cancer. Expressing my raw feelings and thoughts came more easily through the simple words of poetry. Subjects of these entries are primarily about awareness, fears, support and hope.

The photographs are mine as well.

I was very inspired by the following powerful quotes and poetry about grief:

"Grief is a process, not a race. You cannot measure your own grief by somebody else's calendar or rules." Unknown

"Grief is like a journey one must take on a winding mountainside, often seeing the same scenery many times, a road which eventually leads to somewhere we've never been before." Gladys M. Hunt

"In grief, nothing stays put. One keeps emerging from a phase but always recurs. Round and round. Everything repeats. Am I going in circles, or dare I hope I'm on a spiral? But if a spiral, am I going up or down it?" C. S. Lewis

"There is no way around the pain that you naturally feel when someone you love dies. You can't go over it, under it, or around it…Going through is what will help you heal". Therese Rando

"Death leaves a heartache no one can heal. Love leaves a memory no one can steal." Irish Headstone

"Grief comes to stay. It is a new emotion, a new tenant in your heart with a long lease. Grief is as big and as whole as love. It commands attention. It can ruin your day. Grief takes sadness to new heights and throws it off the cliff. " Christine Silverstein

"Imagine having everything that matter. Imagine it gone" Jacqueline Lapidus

TRANSITION

Like birthing midwives
our loving family
gently assisted
Jay's transition to
his heavenly life

Ravaged by cancer
his earthly cocoon
collapsed and set free
his butterfly soul
to the spiritual realm

POETIC HEALING

Caring the weight
and reality of bereavement
is difficult to explain to others
yet there is a need to voice
the complex emotions

Words on a page as poetry
symbolize a lifeline for me
there are stories to tell
memories to face
and pain to bear

Daily meditation and writing
allow the feelings to emerge
to be recorded and
captured for future
processing and remembering

MORNING/MOURNING RITUAL

Each morning
I sit at my sacred place
ring my bell
and light a candle

Each time
I invite the spirit of Jay
to join me
during this quiet time

Each moment
I pray, read, meditate, write,
deep breathe and
reflect on my life

Each day
my spiritual time
becomes
a healing ritual

DREAD

Fear laid silently
in the back of my mind
with each visit
to the doctor

Jay's positive and hopeful
attitude kept me
optimistic and held
my fears at bay

I cherish my moments
spent with this wonderful man
each day
each hour

each minute

FULFILLNESS

Grieving
like pregnancy
cannot be hurried

Each stage
challenges the heart
produces huge shifts

Sorrow
like morning sickness
signals newfound change

Finally
after enduring months
new life emerges

NAVIGATING

Traversing the chasm
between pain and pleasure
seems insurmountable

The vastness of the space
forces me to withdraw
I cannot bridge the gap

The immense distance
appears beyond my reach
and stifles my attempts

Each day my caring friends
take my hand and lead me
on the path of healing

Their tender love and strength
lessen the expanse of pain
and guide me toward living

STARKNESS

My withered heart
lives in dry soils
of emptiness

Every parched cell
longs for waters
of nourishment

Showers of caring
become droplets
of happiness

My thirst is quenched
with healing streams
of growth

SURVIVAL

Treading under the surface
of deep waters of grief
I try to catch my breath
and surface for air

Feeling the heavy weight
of the pain of my loss
my lungs are tightly squeezed
by raw emotions

I frantically inhale
the life-giving forces
of buoyancy and
hopefulness

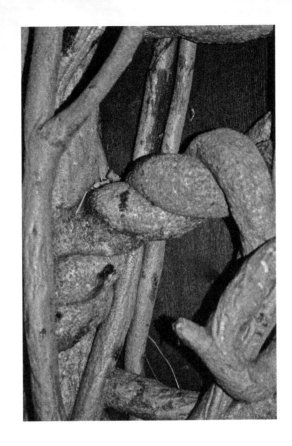

ROOT BOUND

Grief is binding me tightly
like confined roots in a pot

My strands of raw emotion
wind together and coil

When the core of my feelings
twist as much as feasible

It will be time to repot
and allow me to blossom

WIDOWHOOD

My soul mate is gone
I'm a widow NO!
I don't want to be alone
I 'm not prepared to let go

Through his years of sickness
was I preparing for his death
Could I face the reality
of the extent of his cancer

I was blinded by his hope
and on-going optimism
as long as he was fighting
I was at his side with faith

FEARFULNESS

The depth of my love for Jay
is mirrored by the extreme
despair I feel over this loss

I'm blessed to have experienced
Jay's unconditional love
his gentle and accepting
kind heart

Now I struggle to survive
No appetite
No sleep at night
Nothing seems right

I desperately miss him
and search everywhere
hoping for a sign
that his spirit is near

MEMORIES

Images of Jay
fill my mind
drawing me back
to forgotten
memories

Reliving events
brings limited joy
reminding me
of our moments
together

Then sadness creeps in
and the reality
of loss is made clear
leaving feelings
of emptiness

CONDOLENCES

When I hear the words,
It will get better or
God wanted Jay to be with him
I want to scream!
Have you really noticed
how I feel at this moment

I know you may be uncomfortable
and need to fix my loss
You may try to minimize my pain
or feel the need to prescribe
ways for me to conduct myself
You might need to deny my suffering

I'm aware that you mean well and intend no harm
Yet, remember I am not living in my head
but am swimming in deep emotions
I need you to recognize my loss
Saying nothing and being there really do help

DARKNESS

Every evening
I come face to face with
oppressive forms of darkness
not only the night's gloominess
but the bleakness
of my aching heart

My eyes fill with tears
as I try to suppress
the pain of my loss
and relax into sleep
only to awaken
during the night

Sleep provides escape
from the agonizing reality
of Jay's absence and restores
my body to face and
renew my journey

CONNECTION

Everyday I am contacted
by family or by friends
whose caring acknowledgements
provide elements of healing

The panic sense of aloneness
and fear of isolation
prevent me from believing
I will again live a rich life

Then weeks later I discover
loving words of support
that offer glimmers of hope
to buoy up my heavy heart

HEAVINESS

Sadness hangs heavy
around my shoulders
like a massive weight

Held down by deep grief
my lonely heart aches
and longs for relief

Each day looms long
with tough challenges
and new stumbling blocks

No escape nearby
my heart seeks comfort
from supportive people

SURPRISES

The day was dark and gloomy
showers off and on
creating a mood matching
my feelings of despair

Suddenly the doorbell rang
standing at the threshold
was my friend Cindy
holding a bouquet of roses

The smile on her face and hug
gave me a moment of happiness
in the midst of my intense pain
I was surprised by joy

I discovered that
little things provide pleasure
music, kind words, smiles
phone calls and cards

Healing may be possible

MISSING

People, picture, places
all generate
precious memories

Although greatly welcomed
they remind me
of what's missing

Strong waves of loneliness
wash over me
and blur my vision

POWER OF BEING

It's difficult to admit
my attention has focused
on my significant loss

After hearing the author
of the book *Proof of Heaven* speak
I am thinking about Jay

The past two years were tough
with too many days of his fatigue
and lack of energy

Yet he kept soldiering on
and doing what he loved
until he could no more

Now he no longer suffers
I picture him as a happy soul
experiencing pure joy

GRACE

Tears softly fall down my cheeks
as I attempt to find comfort and
solace with the loss
of my beloved husband

Writers speak of *Fierce Grace*
the opening up in a painful
unexpected way
to be a blessing for my life

Is it part of my evolution
as both a human being and
a spiritual being
to face *what is* and dance

MENTORS

I was never prepared
to travel through
wild and dark places

This journey captures
and propels me
into unknown territory

Being caught by the waves
of pain and emptiness
I fear being completely crushed

People who traveled before me
create a map for this passage
pointing to hope and possibilities

QUESTIONS

During my saddest moments
my insecurities arise
I bombard myself with
a multitude of questions

Did I do enough for him?
Did I adequately focus on him?
Was I supportive enough?
Did I allow him to share?
Did I ask the right questions?
Did I miss something he said or did?

The need to go backward
and do things differently
heightens my feelings
of guilt and regret

VULNERABILITY

Always the caretaker,
I find it difficult, yet necessary
to allow others to take care of me
during this period of grief

A note from a friend reminded me
of the challenges of being vulnerable
as well as the rewards

"Nancy, When my life was heavy,
you helped me with a burden.
When my life was dim,
you encouraged me to light it again.
When I needed a friend,
you've been there for me
to show me a new path of possibilities.
With Love, Pat"

TRANSFORMATION

As if in a shell
I'm walled in by grief
detached from the world

Painful emotions shield
my anguishing heart
from feeling happiness

Slight changes occur as
lessened pain permits
some pleasure in living

My butterfly heart
slowly emerges
and begins to open

PASSAGE

The death of my loved one
is the precise moment
when my journey began

Feeling quite abandoned
half-rooted in the past
half-floating into the future

I'm surrounded by grief
on an unfamiliar path
and lost in darkness

Where do I find my guide
In which direction do I turn
What is my destiny

UNCERTAINITY

Through my loss
I am gaining incredible insights
although focusing on what is missing
I face an unknown and lonely future

New directions
fill me with great fear and anxiety
yet recently I've come
to better understand

it's not fear of the unknown
that I am experiencing
it's the fear of losing
what I already have

SOLO JOURNEY

No one says goodbye
as I leave on a trip
Traveling all alone
I rely on myself

No one at home to miss
No one at home to call
No one at home to check in with
No one to whom I return

This solo life trip
no longer a joint venture
leaves me empty
renders me sad

FACES OF GRIEF

This uninvited visitor
is reluctant to leave
and keeps showing up
for more encounters

This uncharted journey
finds me unprepared
to go forward alone,
to face life by myself

I soon discover
it is not a single happening
but an ongoing process
an unpredictable ache

This powerful force,
thrust me to the threshold
of a new pathway
a new beginning

DRIFTLESS

My sails are flapping
in the calm wind
the ropes are lax
the boat is aimless.

From where does wind
and courage come?
Where do I find my way?
What direction am I heading?

Who is my captain?
Is there a course,
a map of navigation
I must take?

SILENCED

My mind is stilled
anxious moments
suspended in midair
as sudden changes
require new thoughts

Life patterns
familiar and routine
that glided me
along well-worn
yet happy paths
disappear

An incredible
radiant life being
someone I
dearly loved
fell forever
silent

EMPTYNESS

I feel like an empty bowl
since the bright sunshine
disappeared from my life

What do I do now
with the empty bowl?
Do I fill it up?

Keep it empty for awhile?
Is there any hurry
to refill the bowl?

CHANGING NATURE

Like works of nature
I am affected
by blowing winds of change

My consciousness is
molded and shaped
by unexpected storms

Like bending trees
I am forced
to adapt and survive

My challenging path ahead
is constantly changing
by flash floods of living

PATH

In the past six months I've found
in grief there is nothing to fight
except feelings of hopelessness

I may sink into the past
freeze, get stuck and remain
recoiled from my painful loss

I grab onto the future
desperate to escape my sorrow
and quickly create a new life

Yet, healing occurs in the moment
where I face what arises
or with great courage
what doesn't

MEDITATION

Early morning walk
leads me through the labyrinth
of tall grasses separating
the roughly mowed path

Brightly colored wildflowers
peek their budding heads
as warm morning sun
washes my face

Overhead birds
sing their cheery songs
and dew clings to the grass
squishing in my toes

This walking meditation
brings music to my soul

HEALING NATURE

Surrounded in nature
I find a place to reflect
by gentle movements of water
haunting sounds of birds

Cool breezes touch my face
rising sunlight warms my skin
swaying branches dance for me
with signs of continuous life

These special gifts of nature
offer promise and hope
by bringing healing elements
to a sad and lonely heart

RENEWAL

The quiet hush of nature
clears my troubled soul
offering healing powers
of natural beauty

Out here in the wilderness
hopefulness runs deep
and assurance of new life
brings renewed energy

TRANSFORMATION

During the grief period
life resembles the journey
of the caterpillar
responding to nature's voice

Time to build a cocoon
leave the old familiar life
spend time in total darkness
where changes can occur

The design is underway
to become a new creature
like the fresh butterfly
find a clear pathway toward light

BACKWARD

Desiring to go back
before the illness
I clearly remember
no rewinds exist

My task as survivor
is working between
the paradox of loss
grieving and cherishing

I need to appreciate
my new life now
No repeating the past
No controlling the future

WAITING

Sad and lonely
I wonder about
day after day
through sorrow and grief

Patiently I wait
to discover
the other side
of emptiness and loss

CLEANSING

Feelings of chaos
fill my surroundings
disarray heightens
my feelings of turmoil

Two special friends
join in the task
pitch in and remove
the immense clutter

The cleansing process
is invigorating
especially with the energy
and love of friends

HOME?

When I sold my Wisconsin house
a friend asked
where is your home

It took me awhile to respond

Home is not a place for me
Home was where Jay was
Home was Jay
When Jay died
I lost my home I said.

Will a house become my home again?

FAREWELL

Up north at Kaubashine Lake
family and friends gather
to spread his ashes in the lake

Clear skies and warm air
provide a perfect atmosphere
for our loving ceremony

Kind words accompany
each special memory
as we scatter his remains

Quiet reflections
of all those present
share thoughts of our loved one

WANDERER

Like a vagabond
I wander from place to place
drifting from home to home
displaced from my nest

Kind friends open up
their arms and homes
offering me respite
from my homeless life

Feeling all alone
driftless and unsettled
I welcome the chance
to be in one place

My nomadic life
will come to an end
when I travel back
to my winter home

DISBELIEF

Months from my terrible loss,
feeling stronger and more focused
I find pockets of joy and peacefulness

Suddenly out of nowhere
blindsided by a wave of grief
I'm sucked underwater again

Frantically I grasp for air and
force myself into calmer waters
struggling to get my bearings

Exhausted and overwhelmed
I try to regain equilibrium
to find my new balance once again

HEALING SOURCE

Every time I have *grief bursts*
I feel my mountain of mourning
too high to ascend again

The deep holes of sorrow
too treacherous to navigate
have returned again

Is there a possible way through

In the midst of my sudden pain
I am amazed I can recover
and regain my balance

Something deep inside of my soul
hungers for comfort and release
arising from my strong faith

CHANGED

Leaving my small shell of solitude
is a very frightening experience
but in the quiet of my comfortable nest
I easily and freely express my pain

I know I cannot continually live
in complete and entire isolation
still my solitary escape from the outside
protects me from my vulnerability

Stepping out of my secure comfort zone
thrusts me into a once familiar world
where scenery and people remain the same
yet I see differently

my life is altered forever

EMPTINESS

Silent are the lonely
for they alone
feel the pain
of emptiness

past the laughter
of children
and the warm
embracing of couples
that remind them
of their loss

HARMONY

Focusing on my experience of loss
thrusts my life out of harmony
as my imbalance is only temporary
and I long to restore equilibrium

I cannot remain hopeful when unstable
so I turn to sources around me for answers
my Divine guidance and continuing support
reestablish balance in my life

FLOW

Just for today
I've decided to give up concerns
about my future
fear nothing
live my life in the present moment
be a part of everything now
become aware without words
feel the ceaseless flow of energy
enjoy the love and joy
from special people
absorb the beauty nearby
feel the warmth of the sun
and cool breezes
appreciate the moon and stars
be swallowed up by
the vibrant life around me

TRAVEL PLANS

The vacations we planned together
road trips, train rides, boat excursions
are no longer on the horizon

Time to shift gears
reshape my dreams
recast my future

As I ponder the road ahead
and greet each day as its own gift
I am discovering what life holds now

TWISTS

Grief propels me on a spiral path
as healing does not happen
in a straight line

Challenges continue along the way
and shadows lurk around every bend
waiting to grab hold again

Fortunately traces of happiness
occasionally appear ahead
on the road to my future

LIVE NOW

As I examine myself
after months of great turmoil
I'm aware that my sharp pain
is no longer all-consuming

When my foundation was shaken
I thought I couldn't survive
I understood where I was
but misplaced my sense of place

I'm aware at many levels,
I will not *get over my deep loss*
I cannot repeat the past
nor can I control the future

I know I must make the best
of my unwanted situation
I am trying now to live
in the precious, present moment

FUTURE

Aware of my fragility
lost in darkness with no escape
I feel trapped and paralyzed
in unknown territory

I'm unable to leave my past
and step beyond the borders of grief

I must embark on my pursuit
to create a healthy future
yet, never, ever forget
the love that encompassed my world

BARRIERS

Traveling for months on my grief journey
I ponder wise words of the sages
Don't identify with what you don't have
Happiness is not other dependent

They're not easy to grasp when in pain
How will I break through the grief barrier
How do I step beyond the edge of loss
How can I construct a rewarding life

CROSSROADS

New life stages are challenges
forced to face ourselves
raise questions about the future
restore our past dreams

Often we've been taught to question
to find our true selves
Yet is that the real process
to find what is unseen

Perhaps as great writers imply
our path is a question
What do we want? What is our dream?
What directs our lives?

At this pivotal stage of life
roads seem uncertain
It's up to me now
to create a grateful person

CHANGE

Change, ever present,
challenges the soul
With change comes loss
that creates imbalance

Losing the familiar
brings sadness and grief
Pain that surfaces
is healed over time

Change,
always difficult
spares no one
Yet it offers new perspectives
inspires new beginnings

PEACE

Listening to an aching heart
a friend offers
comfort and caring

Words frantically erupt
in search
of understanding

Warm gentle responses
wrap around sadness
lifting it away

Peacefulness seeps into
inner cavities
of my broken heart

STRUGGLES

I have learned
to depend on others
for courage and wisdom
on life's journey

I cannot travel alone

When struggling
I need guidance
from those
who really care

SURRENDER

Recognizing things are out of control
I must accept what is
Life becomes chaotic when I insist
on controlling it
I know the outcome I deserve
the pain I feel
Being vulnerable and open-minded
gives me energy
Surrendering to the situation
offers me hope
Approaching the problem with love,
not power
provides necessary distance from
what might have been

CONTEMPLATION

Sitting
my active mind
hears
undesired voices

Waiting
I attempt to
discover
total silence within

Finally
with pen in hand
I enter
writing meditation.

CERTAINTY

Life
a fragile existence
perched on the edge
of a precipice
shows us
nothing is permanent

Suddenly
without any warning
death abruptly comes
causing anguish
that reminds us
life is precious

Eventually
a rainbow appears
following the
unexpected storm
to fill the void
with memories and hope

LIFE SPARK

People like fires
begin as a spark
grow with proper nourishment
crackle and sparkle
blaze with energy

Finally flames subside
brightness turns faint and dim
then to ashen white
until the spark
ceases to be

BELONGING

Friendship
a wonderful connection with people
affords a sense of belonging

Bonds
quickly form to sustain life
and nourish the soul

Support
allows honest exploration of
darkness and brokenness

Openness
clears cobwebs of fogginess
to offer new horizons

Real friends
in the moment of pain
present a vision of reality

CPSIA information can be obtained
at www.ICGtesting.com
Printed in the USA
BVHW021433210219
540827BV00028B/3493/P